Introduction

This 96-page resource book provides specific strategies and activities that will help students learn how to publish a newspaper. Developing a school newspaper not only stimulates students' interests and enthusiasm for writing, it also presents numerous opportunities to teach a variety of writing skills, both creative and practical.

As students complete the newspaper activities and work through the process of publishing a newspaper, they use or reinforce the following writing skills:

Factual, narrative writing	**Writing directions**
Creative writing—stories and poetry	**Conducting and writing interviews**
Letter writing	**Conducting and writing surveys**
Cause-and-effect writing	**Persuasive writing**
Writing opinions	**Descriptive writing in many forms**

The lessons in *Publishing a Newspaper* are designed to increase vocabulary and reinforce basic writing and general language arts skills. The activities also extend to other curriculum areas, such as art (Art Critic, Comics, Advertisements), social studies (career awareness, To the Editor, Travel Sections), math (Survey Statistics, TV Program Schedules), and health (Cure-Alls, Warnings). Furthermore, students express their creativity and artistic abilities in a variety of ways. Each lesson follows the basic writing process, has been classroom tested, and has been found to be successfully applicable in grades 4 through 8.

Since the writing process is employed throughout this resource book, students are constantly exposed to techniques not only for writing but also for responding to each other's compositions. This gives students the opportunity to work with their peers by offering suggestions for how to improve each written composition. Based on this response, the composition is edited and revised, or "remolded." The ultimate goal of this process is a well-written final draft of which the author can be proud and that will be shared with others through publication.

Suggested computer software to use with IBM & compatibles (3.5" and 5.25" diskette) for publishing a classroom newspaper is *The Children's Writing & Publishing Center,* The Learning Company, 6493 Kaiser Drive, Fremont, CA 94555.

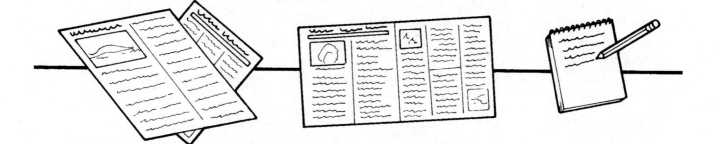

How to Use This Book

Publishing a Newspaper is organized as follows:

- **Introduction** — gives an overview of the coverage and objectives of this book.

- **The Writing Process** — explains the process and describes implementation of it. Use the information and activities on pages 5–6 to introduce or review the steps in the writing process.

- **Writing Process Activities** — are suggested activities that emphasize and support the writing process. Pages 7–27 can be used to supplement or reinforce each step of the writing process: pre-writing, writing, responding, revising, and editing.

- *Stewart Star Reporter* — is a sample newspaper for presenting students' contributions for publication. Students can work together in groups or as a class to complete the lessons and use the blank newspaper format provided on pages 31–38 for writing and illustrating their articles. The sections presented in the *Stewart Star Reporter* are the same as the sections addressed in the student activity pages of this book. As students complete each set of writing activities, use the newspaper as a teaching and/or reinforcement tool.

  (If you prefer, the *Stewart Star Reporter* can be used as a culminating activity.)

- **Glossary of Newspaper Terms** — acquaints students with important newspaper terminology.

- **Newspaper Press Passes** — are worn by students when they conduct surveys or collect materials for reporting.

- **Teacher's Guide** — is devoted to pre-writing activities and experiences, examples for students to model as they proceed with the activities, and extension ideas for using the student pages. The Teacher's Guide is presented on pages 41–50.

- **Student Activities** — introduce the general organization of a newspaper. Throughout the unit, students will need access to newspapers. As an introduction, they should spend some class time looking through a variety of papers and comparing the sections.

The student activities provided on pages 51–96 allow students to experience the writing process using a newspaper format. Students will reinforce and improve their writing skills as they complete activities that focus on several sections (see Table of Contents) of the newspaper.

A writing checklist can be utilized as a guide for the activities in each section. As students complete the activities in this book, review the lessons by having individuals or groups of students share their writing experiences.

The Writing Process

Pre-Writing

Activities that precede writing are vital to any successful writing program. A writer must activate his or her thought processes and creativity before actually forming a draft. Some writers require more preparation than others, and the requirements will vary according to the topics. However, all writers benefit from this sort of beginning search. The pre-writing activities provided in this book can be used on their own to build preparatory skills, or they can be utilized as the initial stages of a specific writing project.

Writing a First Draft

Through pre-writing, the author develops a store of information to use. Now writing is ready to begin. It is the step of the process where form takes place as information is filtered and shaped to meet the author's intentions. The ideas are made to connect with an audience. Writing calls for focus and structure — the narrowing of pre-writing generalities to specifics. However, content, not mechanics, is the prime concern. Activities that foster this approach can be found in this book.

Responding

It is sometimes difficult for a writer to know how other people interpret what he or she has written. Therefore, it is helpful to have an audience provide direction to the author in the process of writing. This is done through reader response. The author can more readily get across what he or she intends by understanding the message the audience is receiving. Reader response can be managed in many ways. Peer response sheets, partner meetings, and writing circles are some of the best. Additionally, some activities simply lend themselves to response.

Revising

So often a student puts something on paper and loathes to alter it in any way. To that student, revising means fixing mistakes and recopying. Yet the student who has real ownership of a composition will be as excited by the revision as by the initial writing. Revision is not slashing with a red pen to mark what is "wrong", but rather remolding to specify exactly what one wants to say.

Editing

Editing and revising go hand in hand. To distinguish between these two steps, an analogy can be made. If the writing were a car, revision would be handled by the design engineer and editing by the mechanic. One designs and shapes while the other repairs and maintains. An important point for you, the teacher, to remember at this stage is that it is not your job to edit. Forget "correcting" student writing. Your job as teacher is to comment, give feedback, and, eventually, to evaluate and grade. However, the composition and all of the steps of the writing process belong to the author.

1. Pre-writing includes:

surveys	experiences	mapping
drawing/art	observations	brainstorming
films	drama	questioning
interviews	patterning/modeling	rich environment
stories	discussing	dialogues

2. First draft writing includes:

journals	reports	letters
learning logs	lists	notes
narratives	descriptions	interviews
summaries	stories	reviews

3. Reader response can be given by:

teacher	small group
partner	whole class

4. Revising includes:

reworking a sentence/paragraph/composition with consideration for organization, clarity, unity, emphasis, or word choice

5. Edit by:

proofreading
combining sentences
using an editing checklist

6. Recopy by:

writing a final draft

7. Follow-up includes:

illustrating	sharing
posting	displaying
publishing	pen pals
contests	awards

Note: Although each lesson plan describes the implementation of the complete writing process, all steps are not always necessary or possible. Teachers need to use discretion as to when the entire process is to be followed.

Contributing Author
Dona Herweck Rice
(*Write All About It!* series)

Editor
Janet Cain, M. Ed.

Editorial Project Manager
Karen Goldfluss, M.S. Ed.

Editor-in-Chief
Sharon Coan, M.S. Ed.

Art Director
Elayne Roberts

Cover Artist
Larry Bauer

Imaging
Hillary Merriman

Product Manager
Phil Garcia

Publishers
Rachelle Cracchiolo, M.S. Ed.
Mary Dupuy Smith, M.S. Ed.

Publishing a Newspaper

Grades 4–8

Author

Marjorie Wein Belshaw, M.A.

Teacher Created Materials, Inc.
6421 Industry Way
Westminster, CA 92683
www.teachercreated.com

©1996 Teacher Created Materials, Inc.
Reprinted, 2002

Made in U.S.A.
ISBN-1-55734-209-1

Table of Contents

Surveys

Several sides of a topic can be investigated by conducting a classroom, school-wide, or take-home survey. Opinions held by a diverse group of people can be gathered and then analyzed by a student or group in writing.

The class or a small group can plan the questions that they believe will cover the topic they are studying. The questions should be as unbiased as possible. For example, *"Do you feel popularity is a reason why some people are elected to the Student Council?"* is a better phrased question than, *"Do you think it is fair that popularity is a reason why some people are elected to the Student Council?"* Survey questions are phrased for short answers, particularly *yes* or *no*. However, because of their restricted form, surveys do not allow for much freedom.

Below is a sample survey that the class can conduct just for fun. Have students use notebook paper to make three copies of the survey. Each student gets a response from one adult, one child, and him/herself. Each responder initials the response sheet.

Question	Response
1. Do you have a "best" friend?	
2. What makes a good friend?	
3. Are you a good friend?	
4. What should friends do together?	
5. What shouldn't friends do?	
6. Is it okay to have a lot of good friends?	
7. How long has your longest friendship been?	
8. Can only people be friends?	
9. Do you think animals have friends?	
10. Are you ever too young or too old to have a friend?	

After the surveys are complete, gather together as a class or in small groups and pool your responses. Discuss the results and students' thoughts and feelings about the results. Share your thoughts and feelings, too. If you would like, each student can then do some writing based on his/her findings, thoughts, and feelings about one or more of the questions. Use the form on page 8 to plan your own surveys.

Survey Form

Question		Yes	Maybe	No
1.	Person A			
	Person B			
	Person C			
2.	Person A			
	Person B			
	Person C			
3.	Person A			
	Person B			
	Person C			
4.	Person A			
	Person B			
	Person C			
5.	Person A			
	Person B			
	Person C			
6.	Person A			
	Person B			
	Person C			
7.	Person A			
	Person B			
	Person C			

First Draft Writing Activities

There are two basic types of writing — the practical and the creative. Practical writing encompasses formal matters of communication such as invitations, business letters, notes of appreciation, consumer complaint letters, thank-you notes, and friendly letters. Each has a structured format that must be followed, leaving little room for creativity. Creative writing, on the other hand, is a unique and novel expression of self. Words are explored and manipulated, analogies are drawn, comparisons are made, and word pictures are set down on paper.

Further division of these two types of writing yields four distinct writing styles or purposes. The chart below describes each and provides sample activities.

Descriptive writing employs details to tell about a given subject. • Describe someone you admire. • Tell about a place you go to be alone. • Describe a video game you like to play. • Write a poem about your favorite toy. • Write a description of the classroom. • Describe someone who annoys you. • Write a lost and found ad for a pet. • Describe your hero.	**Analytical** writing explains how to do something and analyzes people and things. • Write a commercial for a new product. • Tell how to make a taco. • Explain some causes of pollution. • Write a book review. • Define the word *friend*. • Tell why you liked a particular movie. • Explain what happens to old bicycle tires. • Tell how to solve a math word problem.
Narrative writing tells what happened; feelings are shared. • Create your own fairy tale. • Tell about a time when you felt lost. • Tell how you learned to roller skate. • Tell what it means to be well liked. • Write captions for a cartoon. • Tell about your biggest mistake. • Tell about a time you were helpful. • Write a story telling how you failed.	**Persuasive** writing involves getting others to understand and believe in your point of view. • Write a letter to the editor. • Tell why people should stop smoking. • Write an ad for a new product. • Tell why you are for/against an issue. • Create a slogan for your class. • Tell the pros and cons of class rules. • Make a comic to share an opinion. • Tell why something is fair or unfair.

During this first draft writing phase, attention should focus on writing in a logical manner, not just the mechanics (spelling, capitalization, punctuation).

Descriptive Writing

Some sample techniques to encourage descriptive writing are outlined below.

Character Descriptions

Start by making a statement about a chosen subject. Then add details to support the main idea. Students can write a descriptive paragraph or story based on the details listed.

John Henry was an extraordinary man.
He put out the dynamite fuse with his hammer.
He could hammer faster than a steam drill.
He was born with a hammer in his hand.

Sense-able Word Banks

Make a chart with a space for each of the five senses. Have students brainstorm words that fit each category; encourage them to add to the chart after the brainstorming. Provide students with simple sentences. Direct them to rewrite each sentence so that it gives a detailed description.

See	Hear	Taste	Touch	Smell
shadowy	roaring	chocolaty	slimy	burnt
foggy	chirping	sour	sticky	stale
vivid	tiptoeing	creamy	rigid	moldy

Before and After

Provide students with interesting pictures from magazines or newspapers. Delete any captions. Ask students to describe what is happening in the picture. Next, ask them what they think happened before the picture was taken. Then explore what they think will happen next.

Before	Next
Mom put Baby to bed.	Mom will come and comfort Baby.
Baby dropped his bottle.	Baby will fall out of his crib when trying to get his bottle.

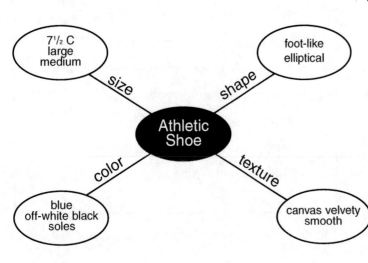

Physical Traits

After determining a topic, write words that describe the size, shape, color, and texture of the object. Use these words to write a vivid, descriptive paragraph.

Narrative Writing

This page contains three narrative writing assignments that will help students write articles for their newspapers and provide additional practice as they complete the student activity pages.

Innovations

Have students start with a familiar story and write innovations of it. Folk tales and fairy tales work well for this activity. As students retell the story, they may want to change the setting, characters, or actions. Remind them to substitute new nouns, verbs, and adjectives to fit the changes they have made. Have students create new titles and draw illustrations for the stories.

Captions

Direct students to bring cartoon strips from the comics section of a Sunday newspaper. Help them eliminate the dialogue by cutting it out or covering it with correction fluid. Tell students to rewrite the story by creating new dialogue. Follow up with this activity: Pair students and give each pair a copy of the storyboard on page 12. Have students cut out and glue the strips together to form one long strip. Instruct them to draw a character in each space. If desired, comic book characters or stickers can be cut out and used instead of illustrations. Then have students write captions for each segment.

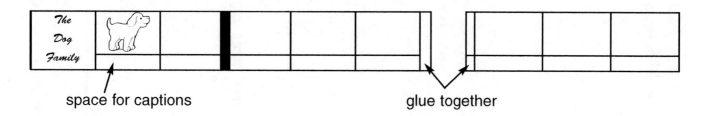

space for captions   glue together

Feelings

In this exercise, encourage students to share their feelings. Brainstorm a situation with students. Some possibilities are listed below on the left. Record the responses on the chalkboard, chart paper, or an overhead transparency. Have students write a story about how they would feel if they were in that situation. A sample brainstorming session appears on the right.

How would you feel if . . .

    . . . your best friend was angry with you?

    . . . everyone in class ignored you?

    . . . you went to a new school and no one would be your friend?

    . . . you learned to snow ski after ten lessons?

> *How I would feel if everyone in the class was invited to a party except me:*
>
> | | |
> |---|---|
> | *unwanted* | *friendless* |
> | *helpless* | *disappointed* |
> | *like crying* | *angry* |
> | *desperate* | *ashamed* |
> | *sad* | *like it was my fault* |
> | *unloved* | *why me?* |

Captions Storyboard

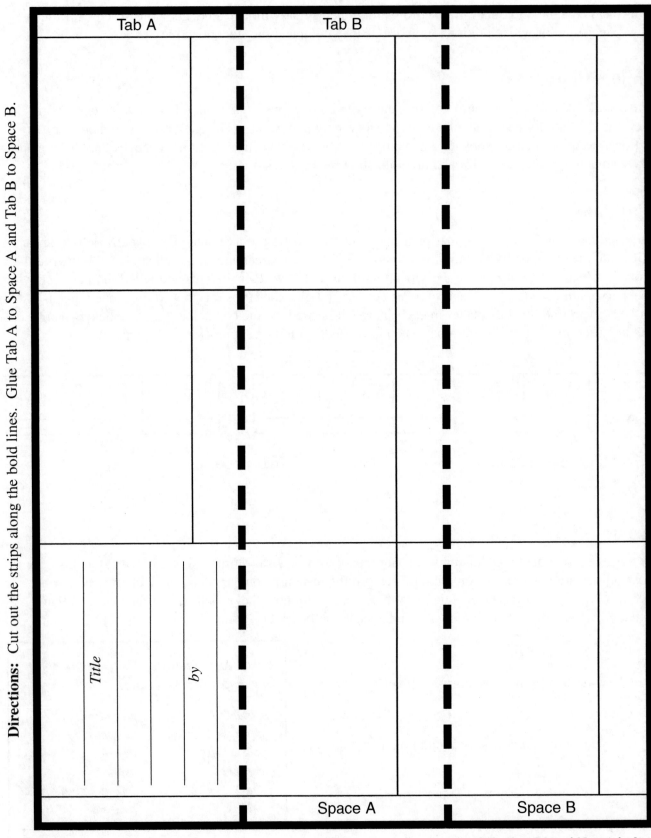

Tab A

Tab B

Title

by

Space A

Space B

Analytical Writing

Teach students how to explain a process and how to analyze a subject with the following exercises.

Flow Chart

A flow chart forces students to think clearly and analyze a process step by step. Skills needed for logical thinking are used to determine what comes next in the process. Model this activity with students before they begin work on their own. One example is shown below. A flow chart form can be found on page 14. This activity should be followed by a corresponding written sequential paragraph. Room for this is provided at the bottom of the flow chart form.

The Water Cycle
1. The sun evaporates water from oceans, seas, lakes, rivers, and streams.
2. The water condenses and forms clouds.
3. Precipitation—rain, hail, snow, sleet—falls from the clouds.
4. Water flows back to the oceans, lakes, rivers, seas, and streams.
5. The cycle continues with number 1 above.

There are four distinct steps in the water cycle. First, the sun evaporates water from sources such as oceans, seas, lakes, rivers, and streams. This evaporated water condenses or compacts to form clouds. Then the clouds create and release various forms of precipitation, such as rain, hail, snow, and sleet. Finally, water from the freshly-filled streams flows back into rivers, and the rivers flow into lakes and oceans. This brings the cycle back to the beginning where it starts all over again.

Define It

Write an unfinished sentence on the board. Have students supply a number of endings. For example, *A friend is someone . . . who cares; who likes you for who you are; who thinks about your feelings.* Direct students to write a paragraph that defines *friend*. Other subjects to define include *happiness, being healthy, love, a perfect day, the best pet, a terrible nightmare,* and *a good citizen.*

A Review

Students can voice their opinions and support them with reasons in book, movie, or article reviews. You may want to model how to write a review before assigning this activity. Make an overhead transparency of page 15 and proceed to review a book, film, or article with which all students are familiar. Provide students with their own copies of the page and have them complete their own reviews of the same book, film, or article. Share the results in small groups.

Flow Chart Form

Title

↓

↓

↓

↓

↓

Write your paragraph on the lines below. Use the back of this paper if necessary.

_____

_____

_____

_____

_____

_____

Reviews

Name _____ Date _____

A Review of _____

☐ Book   ☐ Film   ☐ Article   ☐ Other

1. One thing I liked about this was _____

    _____

    because _____

    _____

2. Another thing I liked was _____

    _____

    because _____

3. What I liked least about it was _____

    _____

    because _____

    _____

4. The best part was_____

    _____

    because _____

5. It could be improved by _____

6. One thing I would not change is _____

7. I would recommend this to _____

8. My letter evaluation *(circle one)*:   A   B   C   D
                                        Excellent   Good   Fair   Forget It

Persuasive Writing

In order to get others to agree with their points of view, students must supply concrete reasons that support their opinions. The following lessons will provide students with opportunities to express their viewpoints.

Pros and Cons

Before forming opinions, students should know about both sides of an issue. For example, should children over 16 have to go to school? An intelligent, informed answer can only be given after both the pros and cons have been examined. The chart at the right shows some possible answers. After the class has explored the pros and cons of an issue, direct students to write a composition about one or both sides.

Should kids 16 and over have to attend school?	
Pros	Cons
• To succeed in life they need to have advanced skills.	• They could be working and earning money.
• It keeps kids off the streets.	• They should be able to decide what they want to do.
• They get to be with friends all day.	• Some kids are bored at school.
• Parents pay taxes so kids can have schools.	

Advertisements

Show students magazine or newspaper advertisements for toys, clothing, food, and soon-to-be-released movies. With the class, talk about the message that each ad is sending to the reader. Ask students a variety of questions about the ads. Examples: *What makes us want those $150 athletic shoes? Why do we want to be the first to see a new science-fiction thriller?*

Pair or group students. Have them write their own advertisements for a new toothpaste, an improved candy bar, a new movie, a favorite author's long-awaited sequel, or a new toy that promises hours of fun. Encourage illustrations or three-dimensional models of the product for the advertisements. Have each pair present the ad for the new product to the class. Have students vote on which is the most persuasive advertisement.

Dear Editor,

Our class read your newspaper's article about the proposed parking fees at the lake. We feel this is unfair because many families will not be able to afford the $5 entrance fee. That means some of us will not be able to use the park for picnics. Others of us will have no place to swim. Furthermore, . . .

Dear Editor

Most magazines and newspapers contain a page where people can voice their opinions about articles that have been run in previous editions. Not all letters to the editor get published, however. Those with a specific viewpoint supported with well-made points stand the best chance of being printed. Editors like to have both sides of a story represented, so students should not be concerned that theirs is an unpopular view. As a class, send editorial comments to a local newspaper. Read newspapers or magazines regularly to find a cause to write about.

Writing Cartoon Stories

Every picture tells a story — or does it? This storyboard needs the captions to make it complete.
Students can create a story that makes sense to them. Then have small groups or the whole class
compare the storyboards to see the differences and similarities.

Provide students with copies of the storyboard form on page 18 and have them create original
illustrations and text for cartoon stories.

Cartoon Storyboard

_____ (title) _____ by _____ (author)		

Creative Writing

Who Said That?

A great source of creativity is the gift of animation to inanimate objects. For example, if a shoe and a sock could talk, what might they say to one another?

Have students write a dialogue between two normally non-speaking objects that are related to any content area. Encourage them to let their imaginations go. At the top of the page, students should draw illustrations or cut and paste magazine pictures to show their chosen characters.

As an extension, students can learn about puns by incorporating them into dialogue tags. Use the following examples to get students started.

"the pencil said pointedly"

"the hairbrush bristled"

"the tennis shoe squeaked out"

Altered Viewpoints

Point out to students that everyone knows what Goldilocks thinks, what keeps Snow White occupied, and how Jack feels about the beanstalk. But what about the other side of the story? What do the three bears talk about over the morning paper? What is the evil queen's favorite weekend pasttime? How does the giant feel about his home being invaded by the little "Englishman"? Use the following activity to give students the opportunity to use their imaginations and tell a well-known story from a different point of view.

Students can rewrite a fairy tale from the villain's point of view or write a villain's defense for the trial that is convened while the other characters are living happily ever after. A great model for this activity is *The True Story of the Three Little Pigs* by Jon Scieszka (with help from A. Wolf), Penguin Books, 1989.

Classified Ads

It is often challenging for people to compose an ad of limited space that conveys all the information they need to give. Ask students to imagine how much fun it would be to write a "Wanted," "Lost and Found," or "For Sale" ad for a character in a story or a real person in history.

Imagine Laura from *Little House on the Prairie* by Laura Ingalls Wilder (HarperCollins, 1953) advertising that she wants an Indian playmate, Kit from *The Witch of Blackbird Pond* by Elizabeth George Speare (Houghton, 1958) composing an ad to teach swimming lessons, or Juan Ponce de León (real-life Spanish explorer) claiming, "Found: The Fountain of Youth." Students can really stretch their imaginations and extend their knowledge of story characters or historical figures at the same time.

Response Activities

Crazy Creations

This type of writing is created purely from the imagination. There are no facts to check or formats to follow. Each student simply invents something that is his/her own and runs with it—the crazier, the better. There is only one rule: Students must use details to describe their Crazy Creations. The reading audience must be able to form a mental image of what the author has created.

Some possible creations can be made from the following:

- house
- car
- bicycle
- amusement park

- animal
- monster
- article of clothing
- sports equipment

Now for the response. After writing, the author should draw and color the Crazy Creation in full detail. Then the written description should be given to another student. That student should draw the Crazy Creation, based solely on the written description. When finished, have students compare the two drawings. Usually, the closer the match, the better the writing!

Persuasive Letters

Students are often able to identify problems in the school. In this activity, they can choose to do something about those problems.

- First, the class can brainstorm a list of problems.
- Next, have each student brainstorm a list of solutions for one of the problems and then pick the best solution to write about.
- Have students write formal letters to the school principal. In their letters, they should clearly and briefly outline the problem, suggest a solution, and provide details supporting why that solution is best.
- As a class, have students select five or six of the best letters. Send those letters to the principal. You may wish to check with the principal to see if he or she is willing to read all of the letters.
- For the response, invite the principal to your class to discuss the problems and solutions with students.

Extension: Have students choose environmental issues and write letters offering possible solutions to your congressional representatives or the offending parties/corporations. Share the responses with the class.

Response Activities *(cont.)*

Dear Blabby

What might Rumpelstiltskin say if he wrote to an advice columnist? How about Pinocchio, Hansel and Gretel, or the Three Billy Goats Gruff? This is an opportunity for students to display their senses of whimsy and humor. Rumpelstiltskin might complain about his name and how he's always doing terrible things as a result of the frustration he experiences. Hansel and Gretel might ask for advice on non-edible road markers. Stress to students that anything is possible where the imagination is concerned.

However, the activity does not stop there. Once written, the letters are sent to "Dear Blabby" (students simply exchange letters), and "Blabby" writes her/his advice. This is the response to the original letter. The advice itself can be shared aloud and enjoyed by everyone.

Advertising Ambush

Here are the steps for a creative advertising activity:

- Show the class a variety of ads targeted at the students' age group. Have students discuss how the advertisers have made the product appealing (i.e., color, humor, peer pressure, etc.).

- Divide the class into teams. Each team of students dreams up a product targeting their age group (i.e., Incredible Edible Pencils, Insta-Homework, Teacher-Away Spray, etc.).

- Each team uses a piece of poster board to design a color ad, complete with slogan and art work, to "sell" the product to their peers.

- The finished ads are displayed, each with an envelope attached to the reverse side.

- Every student is given three tokens (buttons, beans, play money, etc.) and is instructed that each product costs one token. Students can place one token in each of the different product envelopes that they would be interested in buying.

- Count the tokens to see which advertisements were the most successful. Then discuss why some ads were more effective than others.

Revising and Editing Activities

Modeling

It is not always easy for writers to learn the concepts of revising and editing. They may know that change is involved and the purpose is to make the writing better, but they may not understand the process. It is important that this process be modeled for them — not just once but repeatedly, with different styles of writing, with writing by different authors (including published authors, you, and them), and writing in different contexts.

Provide students with copies of pages 23 and 25 and make an overhead transparency of each page. Begin by discussing the different editor's marks shown on page 23. Tell students they can use this page for reference whenever they are revising and editing any kind of composition. Then read the story on page 25 with students. Model how to use the editor's marks on the story.

Reproduce a short draft of your writing (preferably from an assignment that you are doing with students) onto an overhead transparency or the chalkboard. As a class, discuss the changes in grammar, mechanics, and style that can be made. Make use of the dictionary, thesaurus, and other reference books. Note these changes with colored ink or chalk. If possible, avoid red — it carries very negative connotations for students, and editing should not be seen as negative. Together, revise and edit the work.

Now, provide teams of students (group them in threes or fours) with copies of a paragraph to revise and edit. The paragraph can be obtained from the text of a favorite author, your own writing, or anonymous student writing if you have some from past years or other classes. Allow the teams to revise and edit onto large sheets of butcher paper or the chalkboard. Have the teams share their changes with the class. Compare the results, pointing out that a variety of approaches possible. Stress to students that there is no one best way to revise. Post the original and the changes around the room.

As part of your regular writing program, occasionally revise and edit as a class or in small groups. In addition, provide students with copies of page 24. Ask them to use this checklist to evaluate their own writing. Make revising and editing a natural, expected part of the writing process.

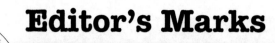

Editor's Marks

You may wish to refer to this page when you are revising and editing a composition.

Editor's Mark	Meaning	Example
ℓ	Delete.	It was ~~was~~ very tiny.
≡	Capitalize.	the boy ran quickly.
/	Make lower case.	Many Athletes ran in the marathon.
∧	Add a word.	ice ∧ sundae (cream)
RO	Run-on sentence	Who's there RO what do you want?
frag.	Sentence fragment	The peddler's cart. frag.
sp	Spelling error	Monkies swung on the tree. sp
∪	Reverse letters or words.	Five books (on were) the shelf.
⊙	Add a period.	The children played ⊙
⋏	Add a comma.	Apples ⋏ peaches, and pears
⌄	Add an apostrophe.	Johns puppy
⌄⌄ ⌄⌄	Add quotation marks.	Help! I cried.
¶	Begin a new paragraph.	"Hello," said Carla. ¶ Hi," Beth replied.
#	Make a space.	French # fries
⌒	Close the space.	country ⌒ side
stet	Do not delete (let what was deleted remain).	the ~~beautiful~~ swan stet

Editing Checklist

1. Did I capitalize all the important words of my title?

2. Did I indent each paragraph?

3. Are my margins correct?

4. Did I capitalize the first word of every sentence?

5. Did I capitalize all proper nouns? (Examples: Tom, Shatoja, Harper School, Monday, Thanksgiving)

6. Did I use the correct punctuation marks?

7. Is each sentence a complete thought?

8. Do most of my sentences in a paragraph begin with a different word?

9. Did I use colorful speech? (Examples: similes, metaphors, idioms, synonyms, personification)

10. Did I use pronouns correctly?

11. Did I use transition words? (Examples: although, because, when, while, therefore)

12. Did I avoid overusing certain words? (Examples: then, so, but, and)

13. Did I avoid using dead words and omit any unnecessary words?

14. Did I spell each word correctly?

15. Is my handwriting legible?

Crazy Cars

The car was one of the strangest Ive ever seen. It had for wheels but they were turned on their sides and moved the car too the left or the rite. The doors were on the back the fron was a bign sheet of tinted glass that curved under and across the botom of the car. You could see the rode as You drove over it. My sister really liked that. And the stearing wheal was more like a tearing pole. Sort of like a joystick. And best ofall, with a flip of the switch this incredibel car would float off the ground. no more traffic jams! It may have been funny but it sure was a lot of fun!

Publishing Activities

Publishing Explained

Publishing is simply the final stage of production for a piece of writing, during which it is put into its completed format with cover, illustrations, author biography, dedication, and/or any other facet the author wishes to include.

There are many ways to publish. Directions and patterns for several methods can be found in this section.

What to Publish

Remember, stories are not the only written works that can be bound into books. Some suggestions are shown below.

- class poetry
- a writing circle anthology
- an individual's anthology
- student newspapers
- author biographies
- plays and skits
- charts and graphs
- journals
- interviews
- storyboards
- modern fairy tales
- student-written song lyrics
- travel brochures
- detective reports
- jokes
- dialogues
- wills

- class brainstorms
- "I am the one who is . . ."
- class likes and dislikes
- story maps
- painted writing
- mini-murals
- picture stories
- illustrations
- sales pitches
- mixed-up fables
- imaginary creations
- original restaurant menus
- recipes
- book reviews
- obituaries
- personalized stationery
- research reports

Publishing Activities *(cont.)*

Organizations that Publish Student Work

Many magazines and papers publish original student work. Contact the organizations below for details about their current publishing standards and submission requirements.

1. Original responses to fiction or nonfiction can be submitted to:

   The Perfection Form Company
   1000 North Second Avenue
   Logan, Iowa 51546

2. Original writings or art from students grades 7 through 10 can be submitted to:

   Merlyn's Pen: National Magazine of Student Writing
   P.O. Box 1058
   East Greenwich, RI 02818-9946

3. Original writings and artwork from students of ages 8–14 can be submitted to:

   The Flying Pencil Press
   P.O. Box 7667
   Elgin, IL 60121

4. Original writings and artwork under an assigned theme or topic from students of ages 5–9, 10–14, and 15 and over can be submitted to:

   Cricket League
   Carus Publishing Company
   P.O. Box 300
   Peru, IL 61354

5. Original writings and art from students through age 13 can be submitted to:

   Stone Soup
   P.O. Box 83
   Santa Cruz, CA 95063

6. Original stories, articles, and craft ideas can be submitted to:

   Highlights for Children
   803 Church Street
   Honesdale, PA 18431

7. Original written and illustrated stories can be submitted to:

   The National Written & Illustrated By . . . Awards Contest for Children
   Landmark Editions, Inc.
   P.O. Box 4469
   Kansas City, MO 64127

Behind the Scenes—Typesetting

The work of all departments and sections comes together in the printing of the newspaper.

This is the job of the **Mechanical Department**. All of the stories, art, and photos must be *typeset*—put into a form for printing. This is a big job. Most modern papers use computers to help them.

Choosing the Font

One of the decisions that must be made before printing is what kind of type—the *font*—will be used. A font is a combination of three things—*typeface, type size,* and *type weight.*

Typeface

The style of type is called typeface. For example, letters may have serifs—small extra horizontal lines.

M⟶SERIFS⟵B

Or, they may be *sans-serif*, without extra lines.

M B

Some common typefaces include: Times Roman (serif), Helvetica (sans-serif), and *Zapf Chancery* (script).

Type Size

Type may be Large, small, or many other sizes. *Type size* is measured in points. One point is very small. Most of the type on this page is 12 point.

Type Weight

Type weight is the thickness and slant of the lines in letters. For example, words may be printed in **boldface**, in *italics*, or in combinations like ***bold italics.***

Try This Match Type Size with "Choosing the Font"

Cut two or more headlines from a newspaper. Copy them onto a piece of paper so you will not forget what they say. Then cut the letters apart. Mix them up. Now reassemble the headlines. Line the letters up straight. This is something like the job typesetters had before machines were invented to help them. Imagine doing this for a whole newspaper!

Find the following in a newspaper:

- three different typefaces
- several sizes of type
- examples of **bold** and *italic* prints

Behind the Scenes — Layout

Deciding where the stories, pictures, ads, etc., will go is called *layout*. Someone must "lay out" the parts of a page to see where they will fit and look good. The arrangement is then glued to a sheet the size of the newspaper's page. This is called the *paste-up*.

Cut on the dark lines of this page. Arrange the pieces on a sheet of paper this size and "paste them up." Draw appropriate pictures or ads for the empty spaces. Compare your arrangement with those of other students. How are they alike, and how do they differ?

MANY CHILDREN HEAD FOR PARKSIDE POOL

Headline

By George Scott

NEW CITY—Students were overjoyed today when the city schools closed for summer vacation.

At 12:00 noon the children left the schools on their way to vacations, swimming, ball games, and all the other pleasures of the long-awaited summer.

At Glenwood School 285 joyful youngsters met in the school auditorium for one last sing-along just before school was dismissed. The favorite song was "In the Good Old Summertime."

Later, Jeremy Holmes was dejected as he waited for his bus. "You'd think it could be on time today of all days!" he exclaimed.

School Is Out!

Banner

By Juanita Lopez

NEW CITY—During the morning of June 22, the last day of school for New City youngsters, Principal Mary Jones visited each class to wish the children a happy and safe summer vacation. Ever the educator, she also encouraged them to read and write over the summer. "It's fun, and you'll remember what you've learned for next fall," said Ms. Jones.

Summer Vacation Begins

Subhead

By Lee Chang

NEW CITY—Five hundred fifty children crowded Parkside Pool on Friday afternoon after city schools were dismissed for vacation. "It could be a long, hot summer," said weary lifeguard John Stewart.

PRINCIPAL JONES VISITS CLASSES TO SAY GOOD-BYE

Headline

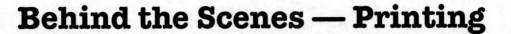

Behind the Scenes — Printing

The paste ups are used to make printing plates which are curved to fit on a large cylinder of a printing press. Paper from huge rolls is pulled through the presses to print the paper in much the same way paper rolls through a typewriter. This happens at a very high speed. Other machines cut and fold the pages.

You Can Print From a Cylinder

Assemble these materials:

- cardboard tube(s) from paper towels or wraps
- heavy string
- water
- white glue
- spoon or stirrer
- scissors
- wax paper
- aluminum foil
- small dish or foil pan
- tempera paints or colored ink
- cookie sheet with sides
- paper on which to print

Follow these directions:

1. Thin some white glue with a little water in the dish. Stir until they are well mixed.

2. Cut the string into short lengths.

3. Dip each piece of string in the glue mixture, making sure it is completely wet.

4. Glue the string onto the cardboard tube in an interesting picture or design. Leave the ends of the tube free to use as "handles." (If you wish to make letters, they must be backwards in order to print correctly. A good way to do this is to write with dark marker on a thin piece of paper. Turn the paper over and copy what shows through to the reverse side.)

5. Put the tube on wax paper to dry.

6. Line the cookie sheet with foil. Spread some tempera paint or ink in a thin layer over the foil.

7. Roll the dried tube in the paint until the string is inked.

8. Now roll the tube on your paper to see your print.

Hint: You can let your tube dry and then add to your print with another color, or you can make a tube for each color you wish to use.

Stewart Star Reporter

Feature Stories—News

Feature Stories—News

Picture

Feature Stories—News

Feature Stories—News

Index

Stewart Star Reporter

Picture

Authors–Poets

Art Critic

Authors–Poets

A selection of stories and poems by _____

_____

Picture

Stewart Star Reporter

Interviews

Interviews

Picture

Letters to the Editor

Letters to the Editor

Stewart Star Reporter

Helpful Hints

Picture

Business News

Recipes

Picture

Cure–Alls

Reviews

Picture

Stewart Star Reporter

Travel

Picture

Survey

Dear Blabby

Dear Blabby

Stewart Star Reporter

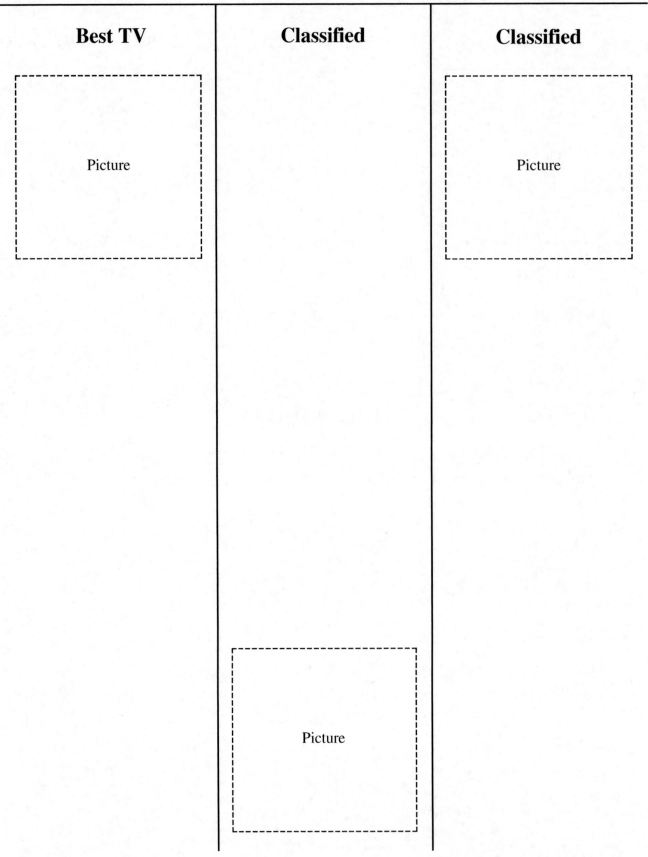

Best TV	Classified	Classified
Picture		Picture
	Picture	

Stewart Star Reporter

Comics

Comics

Advertisements

Sports

Stewart Star Reporter

Puzzle

Warnings	Riddles	Jokes
Picture		
		Picture

Glossary of Newspaper Terms

AP — stands for the Associated Press, a wire news service which provides information to newspapers

Assignment — a specific story to be covered by a reporter

Background — information a reporter must research to understand a story

Banner — a headline with large type that goes all the way across the front page

Beat — the regular assignments, such as school board or city council meetings, given to a reporter

Byline — name of the reporter who wrote the story

Copy — all the words in a newspaper

Cutline or Caption — short phrase that identifies the contents of a photograph, picture, or graph

Dateline — the line at the beginning of a story that tells the location and can also tell the date

Deadline — time by which all stories must be completed and turned in

Dummy — shows the layout of how a newspaper page will look

Editor — the person who reviews stories submitted by the reporters and decides what stories will go into the paper and where they will be placed

Editorial — a column that expresses a personal viewpoint or opinion

Feature — a story written about people's interests, entertainment, etc.

Headline — large type words before or above an article that tell what the article is about (title)

Index — a table of contents for the paper, usually found on the front page

Jumpline — tells where a story is continued

Lead — first paragraph of a story which covers the 5 W's (who, what, when, where, why) and sometimes how

Logo — a slogan, design, or artwork that is the newspaper's trademark

Masthead — goes across top of the front page and tells the name of the newspaper, where it is printed, and the date of issue

Newsprint — the kind of paper used for printing newspapers

Publisher — head of the newspaper, makes important decisions about the paper

Reporter — one who covers current events or writes other kinds of stories for the newspaper

Syndicated Features — anything, such as comics and advice columns, provided by news syndicates to newspapers throughout the nation

Teaser — is often found on the front page and is used to announce an interesting story that appears elsewhere in the newspaper

Wire Photo — a picture that is sent out by telephone wires or satellite to all newspapers that subscribe to this service

Newspaper Press Passes

Reproduce the press passes shown below for students. Have each student fill in the information on a pass and glue a photograph or draw and glue a self-portrait in the corner. Then have students glue the passes onto pieces of tagboard that are cut to the same size. You may wish to laminate the passes. Attach the passes to students' clothing using a metal clip or a clothespin. Students can wear their press passes during interviews and when collecting survey information.

Patterns

Press Pass

Picture

Name: _____

Newspaper: _____

Date of Birth: _____

Height: _____

Weight: _____

Hair Color: _____

Eye Color: _____

Social Security Number: _____

Press Pass

Picture

Name: _____

Newspaper: _____

Date of Birth: _____

Height: _____

Weight: _____

Hair Color: _____

Eye Color: _____

Social Security Number: _____

Teacher's Guide

Lesson 1: The News Story (pages 51-53)

Activity 1—Taking Notes

- Collect, read, and discuss news stories from school news publications and/or daily papers.

- As a class, brainstorm the difference between a fictional story and a news story. List the differences on a chart.

- Discuss with the class the organization of a news story.

- Distribute newspaper articles and copies of Activity 1 (page 51) to groups of students. Have them read the articles within their groups to find the following information and record it on their worksheets. Allow each group to share its findings with the class.

headline	byline	climax
main idea of the story	dateline	details

Activity 2—Writing a News Story

Discuss the common structure of the first two paragraphs of a news story:

Paragraph 1—Organization (begins with climax and states who, what, when, where; then elaborates on the story by explaining why and how)

Paragraph 2—Details (provides more details to support the information provided in the beginning paragraph)

- Prepare students for writing a news story by discussing actual news events that might be used for their articles, or choose an imaginary incident from the following: car crash, fire, arrival of a prominent person, football game, earthquake or another type of natural disaster. Follow these steps:

  1. Allow students to draw pictures of the event.

  2. Discuss and list on a chart or chalkboard good lead lines, such as the following:

  Quotes Example—"The earth shook like a bowl of jelly," exclaimed the woman as she stood by her devastated home after the earthquake.

  Dramatic Word Picture Example—The ground trembled, houses shook, and trees swayed back and forth as the earthquake shook the city of San Francisco.

  Summary Stating the Facts—The death toll is yet unknown but the amount of damage caused by the earthquake that struck San Francisco is estimated in the millions of dollars.

  Question Example—What caused such a devastating fire? Firemen are now investigating the cause of the fire that burned hundreds of homes in the Oakland Hills area yesterday.

  3. Reproduce Activity 2 (pages 52-53) for students. Have them use the format provided on the worksheets to write their own news stories.

Teacher's Guide *(cont.)*

Lesson 2: Author/Poet Corner (pages 54–63)

Writing a Fantasy (pages 54–59)

- Before having students write a fantasy, read several fantasies and choose one for a class teacher-directed lesson on analyzing plots. Use Activity 1a (page 54) to introduce and discuss the basic structure of a fantasy.

- Explore topics students can use for writing fantasies. Some possible topics include ghosts, spells and potions, fairies and elves, wizards, warlocks and witches, animals, unusual beings, magicians, princes and princesses, wicked stepmothers, trolls, giants, and monsters.

- Once the topic has been chosen, help students complete Activities 2a and 3a (pages 55–56). These worksheets focus on developing characters, setting, and other relevant information.

- Have students work independently to complete the outline for Activity 4a (pages 57–59). Then ask them to write rough drafts of their fantasies. You may wish to continue the writing process by allowing time for responding, revising, editing, and publishing.

Writing Poetry (pages 60–63)

- Have available a supply of poetry books that demonstrate a variety of poetry forms. Possible references include:

    Month Poem: *A Child's Calendar* by John Updike (Knopf, 1989)

    General: *A Child's Book of Poems* by Gyo Fujikawa (Grosset & Dunlap, 1969); *Small Poems Again* by Valerie Worth (Farrar, Straus, & Giroux, 1986); *A Child's Garden of Verses* by Robert Louis Stevenson (Philomel, 1990)

- Read and discuss some poems, noting the differences between rhyming and non-rhyming poetry as well as other elements within the poems. Present examples of both types of poetry.

- Guide students as they complete Activities 1b and 2b (pages 60–61). Have them work independently to complete Activity 3b (pages 62–63) then share their poetry with the class. You may wish to feature some students' poems in the *Stewart Star Reporter.*

Lesson 3: Art Critic (pages 64–66)

- Show several famous works of art, both portraits and landscapes. With the class, discuss what to look for in great works of art, such as realism and the use of color to express mood and deeper feelings the artist might want to impart.

- Display and discuss a portrait painted by one of the great masters.

- Have students complete the paragraph frame for Activity 1 (pages 64–65). Tell them to use adjectives to describe the painting and list special features unique to the portrait.

Teacher's Guide *(cont.)*

Lesson 3: Art Critic (pages 64–66) *(cont.)*

- Have students assume the role of art critic as they share their impressions of the painting.

- As a follow-up to this activity, have students collect portraits from other artists and present critiques on the paintings.

- Present a lesson on critiquing landscape paintings for Activity 2 (page 66), using the same procedure as described above for critiquing portraits. Save the most descriptive critiques for the *Stewart Star Reporter.*

Lesson 4: Interviews (pages 67–68)

- Discuss the purpose of an interview.

- Discuss people whom students might interview. Here are some suggestions.

school staff member	police officer	local politician
firefighter	businessperson	sports celebrity

- Reproduce the interview worksheets (pages 67–68) for students and discuss the kinds of questions that should be asked during an interview. Students may wish to add other questions.

- Discuss how to prepare for an interview.

  1. Remind students to be polite at all times.

  2. Point out to students that it is natural to feel nervous when they are talking to someone they do not know. Explain that an interview will go more smoothly if they try to remain calm and are prepared. You may wish to practice some simple relaxation exercises.

  3. Stress the importance of making an appointment in advance.

  4. Tell students that they must be on time for the interview.

  5. Allow time for students to role-play how to ask someone for an appointment, as well as how to conduct the interview.

  6. Point out that the following things should be brought to the interview: worksheets (pages 67–68), sharpened pencil with an eraser; clipboard or book on which to write.

  7. Discuss the need to avoid "yes" or "no" answers by asking questions that begin with *who, what, where, when, why, how.*

- On the basis of the class discussion and the review of the interview worksheets (pages 67–68), students proceed with their interviews. Allow plenty of time for students to complete this assignment since they must accommodate different people's schedules.

- Based on the answers students recorded on their worksheets, instruct them to write the first draft summary of their interviews using complete paragraphs.

Teacher's Guide *(cont.)*

Lesson 5: To the Editor (pages 69–71)

- Discuss what an editorial is: a special type of newspaper article that includes both facts and opinions. Usually it deals with controversial issues that cause strong feelings. The author of an editorial tries to persuade readers to agree with his or her opinion.

- Distribute copies of page 69 as an introductory lesson.

- Ask students to brainstorm a list of topics that are the cause of current concerns. Write students' suggestions on the chalkboard. Some examples are listed below.

violence in our society	overpopulation
graffiti	juvenile crime
communicating with parents	cheating
use of animals for experimentation	homelessness
honesty	benefits of exercise
world hunger	present problems in education
neighborhood gangs	preservation of the environment
controlling communicable diseases	germ warfare
family conflict	traffic safety

- Allow students to choose a topic and give them time to research it by reading about it and/or discussing it with others.

- Discuss the format for a letter to the editor as presented on the worksheets (pages 70–71).

- Instruct students to complete the outline form for their letters. Then have students use their outlines to write the first draft of their three-paragraph editorials.

Lesson 6: Writing Instructions (pages 72–73)

- Discuss how instructions should be written.

  1. As a class, make a paper airplane.

  2. As each step is completed, students should write the instruction for that step.

  3. After the instructions are completed, students check the accuracy of the instructions by using them to construct another paper airplane.

- Tell students to note the importance of beginning with a list of all the materials that are needed to construct something or to complete a task.

- Stress the need for clarity, a logical sequence, and completeness in writing instructions.

Teacher's Guide *(cont.)*

Lesson 6: Writing Instructions *(cont.)*

Invite students to brainstorm a list of topics for which instructions could be written. Some suggestions are provided below.

How to . . .

tie a shoelace	wrap a present	ride a bike
make a pizza	do long division	apply lipstick
change a bike tire	write a report	scramble an egg
bathe a dog	log on a computer	design a greeting card
draw a star	grill a hamburger	write a letter
clean a fish tank	make a sundae	make a bed
write a recipe	make a sandwich	change diapers
braid hair	build a bird's nest	play a game

• Discuss the importance of using illustrations to help clarify the instructions.

• Using the worksheet on page 72, have students write instructions or recipe steps in random order and then put them in the correct sequence by correctly numbering the steps.

• Using the worksheet on page 73, have students write the first draft of their instructions or recipes in paragraph form, using the correct sequence.

Lesson 7: Cure-Alls (page 74)

• Discuss various ailments students have had and the cures that were prescribed.

• Discuss common concerns, as well as strange or comical maladies one could have or contract. List these on the chalkboard. Some suggestions are shown below. Then talk about possible cures for each concern or ailment.

freckles	crooked nose	crossed eyes	indecision
curly hair	jealousy	headaches	easily tired
broken heart	gray hair	crooked teeth	stress
baldness	hiccups	frog in throat	allergies
shyness	old age	indigestion	forgetfulness

• Discuss the essentials for a cure-all ad. Be sure to include the following descriptions: ailment, symptoms, and description of the cure (given in detail).

• Distribute copies of the worksheet on Cure-Alls (page 74). Guide students as they complete their worksheets.

• Using the information on the worksheet (page 74), have students write the first draft of their cure-alls.

Teacher's Guide (cont.)

Lesson 8: Writing Reviews (page 75)

- Discuss what kinds of things or activities may be reviewed.

play	dance performance	band concert	assembly program
movie	book	art exhibit	orchestra concert

- Discuss what a review should include.

  1. Title of what is being reviewed

  2. Author or producer

  3. Place where it can be attended, seen, or acquired

  4. Brief description of characters, performers, or type of artwork

  5. Brief description of the content

  6. Description of the best and worst parts

  7. An evaluation telling why it is or is not being recommended

- Emphasize that a review should tell about the work of art without telling so much as to spoil one's enjoyment of it.

- Instruct students to fill out the worksheet on page 75. Then have them write first draft reviews based on the information on their worksheets.

Lesson 9: Travel Sections (page 76)

- Collect and ask students to bring in travel brochures that describe various vacation areas.

- Using a place that is familiar to all students, work with the class to fill out page 76.

- Instruct students to write the first draft of their three-paragraph travel brochures, based on the information they have written on their worksheets.

- Write the following list of travel words on the chalkboard or a chart. Emphasize that students should use some of these words when writing their brochures.

adventure	cruise	fare	passenger	sightseeing
accommodations	currency	hotel	passport	ticket
airplane	departure	inn	rate	tip
airport	destination	itinerary	recreation	tour
arrival	entertainment	luggage	relaxation	tourist
baggage	exchange rate	motel	reservation	train
bed and breakfast	foreigner	off season	resort	trip
cooking	motor lodge	package tour	round trip	vacation

Teacher's Guide *(cont.)*

Lesson 10: Survey Statistics (pages 77–78)

- Discuss the importance of conducting surveys.

- Set down the following guidelines for making a survey. Select a topic, decide on a question, list the topic choices, ask questions of a number of people, summarize the results.

- Present the sample survey for Activity 1 (page 77) and discuss it.

- Have students brainstorm a list of some possible subjects to use for surveys. (**Suggestions:** trips, school events, pets, TV programs, hobbies, school subjects, popular songs, favorite foods)

- Ask students to select topics to survey. Using Activity 2 (page 78), have students conduct their surveys and write the first draft of their survey reports.

Lesson 11: Advice Columns (pages 79–80)

- Read newspaper articles from "Dear Abby" and other such advice columnists.

- Review the correct form for writing letters and addressing envelopes.

- Discuss the content of the advice column letter. Have students complete Activity 1 (page 79) to write letters to an advice columnist. Tell students the kind of information, as described below, that should be included in their letters.

  Paragraph 1 — State the problem in detail and tell exactly what has happened. Describe what you have tried to do about it.

  Paragraph 2 — State the desire for a solution to the problem. Thank the columnist in advance for his or her suggestions.

- Have students use the information from page 79 to write the first draft of their letters.

- Reproduce Activity 2 (page 80) for students. Discuss how an advice columnist writes a reply letter. Point out the importance of using good judgment and suggesting reasonable solutions when writing a reply letter.

- Have students complete Activity 2 before writing the first draft of their reply letters.

Lesson 12: TV Programs (page 81)

- Study TV guides and daily TV schedules found in newspapers.

- Reproduce page 81 for students and make an overhead transparency of that page. Discuss what kinds of information are necessary and important when planning TV program schedules. Have students pick a show with which everyone is familiar. Use the transparency to guide students as they complete their worksheets.

- Have students use the worksheet (page 81) to record information about a TV program. Instruct students to work together as a class to develop a TV program schedule on the basis of the information on their worksheets.

Teacher's Guide *(cont.)*

Lesson 13: Classified Ads (pages 82–83)

- Discuss the types of ads that are placed in the classified section of the newspaper. Point out that "Job Wanted" ads are part of the classified section.

- Discuss how one might earn $50.00 as soon as possible. List students' suggestions on the chalkboard or a chart.

doing chores	caring for pets
washing cars	delivery person
walking dog	baby-sitting
garden work	garage cleaning
paper boy or girl	presenting a magic or puppet show

- Discuss and outline the information needed to write an effective "Job Wanted" ad:

  1. Services to be rendered

  2. Reasons why the student should be hired or why the student wants the job

  3. Work experience

  4. Additional skills possessed

  5. Statistics: name, age, phone, time available, salary requirements

  6. Two or three references

- Discuss catchy headline phrases or questions that might be used. Some suggestions are provided below.

Excellent Employee	Do you need some time to yourself?
Self-Starter Looking for Work	Are you too busy to do everyday chores?
Is your garden looking shabby?	Do you need someone to care for your pet?

- Instruct students to complete the worksheets (pages 82–83). Then, on the basis of the information on the worksheets, have them write the first draft of their classified ads.

Lesson 14: Puzzles (page 84)

- Allow students to solve several word search puzzles similar to the one they are going to create.

- As a class, compose a word search puzzle. To create the puzzle, you may wish to have students use words from one of the following sources: newspaper terms (page 39); vocabulary from reading, math, social studies, or science; weekly spelling list; frequently misspelled words; or a student-generated list.

- Reproduce page 84 for students. Instruct students to devise their own puzzles using the worksheet.

- Allow time for students to work each other's puzzles.

Lesson 15: Warnings (page 85)

* Read the following to the class: "Warning" and "Early" from *Where the Sidewalk Ends* by Shel Silverstein (HarperCollins, 1974).

* Discuss various types of warnings. You may wish to use the examples provided below.

Always look both ways before crossing a street.	Always tie your shoelaces.
Never use electricity near water.	Do not listen to loud music.
Do not climb a high tree.	Never run with scissors in your hand.

* Discuss the need to include a reason to explain why each warning is important. Present examples, such as the ones shown below. Some can be humorous.

    Don't sit in the sun too long or you will melt.

    Never jump from an airplane without a parachute or you'll end up on the ground looking as flat as a pancake.

* Instruct students to write the first draft of their warnings on page 85.

Lesson 16: Riddles (page 86)

* Read and/or tell numerous riddles.

* Discuss the important information that needs to be given in a riddle: complete physical description, something the person is good at doing and/or for which he/she is famous, something special about the person, when and where he/she lives or lived.

* Reproduce page 86 for students. Help students fill out the worksheet. Instruct students to use their worksheets to write the first draft of their riddles.

Lesson 17: Jokes (page 87)

* Ask students to share their favorite jokes with the class. Remind students that these jokes must be appropriate for school.

* Help students evaluate these jokes and decide on some requirements for a good joke.

* Possible requirements include:

    1. Appropriateness for a school newspaper

    2. Form: topic sentence, build up the sequence of events to a climax or "punch line," punch line.

Have students complete the worksheet (page 87). On the basis of this information have students write the first draft of their jokes in paragraph form.

Teacher's Guide *(cont.)*

Lesson 18: Comics (pages 88–91)

- Collect, read, and study various comic strips. Then discuss the elements of a comic strip: comics must have a plot or problem; the characters and background in comics are illustrations; the text of comics is contained within speech bubbles connected to each speaker.

- Reproduce Activities 1 and 2 (pages 88–89) for students and assign these worksheets.

- Discuss and set up the procedure for writing a comic strip using these steps: **Select** the characters; **decide** on an action or problem; **write** the sequence of events in a logical order; **decide** what kinds of illustrations will show the action of the events; **write** a dialogue to go with the action sequence; **choose** a format for publication.

- Discuss and list possible situations for comics. Suggestions include two ghosts talking; dreams — scary, funny, unusual; circus events; two fish in a fishbowl; and a before and after situation.

- Using Activity 3 (page 90), have students list the characters, name the problem or conflict, and outline the sequence of events for their comics.

- Assign Activity 4 (page 91) to have students create the first draft of their comics.

Lesson 19: Advertisements (pages 92–95)

- Reproduce Activity 1 (page 92) for students. Discuss the principles for designing a good ad and the design vocabulary.

- Use Activity 2 (page 93) to discuss examples of ads. Relate the principles from page 92 to these ads. Do the same for current newspaper ads.

- Distribute and discuss the checklists for Activity 3 (page 94). Stress that all the points named on the checklists are necessary information and should be included in an effective advertisement.

- Have students complete Activity 4 (page 95) to design their own ads.

Lesson 20: Sports (page 96)

- Collect sports sections from several newspapers for the class to read and discuss. As a result of the discussion, lead the class to develop a note-taking form to include the following: name of the event, date of the event, name of the contestants/players, where they played, final score, most exciting moments, and star players.

- Discuss the vocabulary list (page 96) used by sports writers. Add other words if needed.

- Assign students sports events, viewed live or on TV, in order to complete the worksheet (page 96).

- Instruct students to write the first draft of their sports article based on the information they have recorded on their worksheets.

Lesson 1: The News Story

What to Do:

❑ Complete the class pre-writing activities, as directed by the teacher.

❑ Write the first draft of your news story (pages 52–53) about a real or imaginary current event on the basis of the pre-writing activities.

❑ Obtain constructive criticism by having a partner, group, or class respond to your writing.

❑ Revise and edit your writing based on the responses.

❑ Recopy.

❑ Save your news story as a reference for writing articles for the classroom newspaper.

Activity 1—Taking Notes

Choose a feature article from the newspaper. After reading the article, practice taking notes about your article by completing the information below. You may wish to refer to this worksheet as a guide for writing your own news story (pages 52–53).

Headline: _____

Main idea of story: _____

_____

Byline:_____

Dateline: _____

Climax:

    Who? _____

    When? _____

    Where? _____

    What? _____

_____

    Why? _____

_____

    How? _____

_____

Details: _____

_____

_____

Lesson 1: The News Story

Activity 2—Writing a News Story

Choose an exciting or interesting event that has occurred recently or that you have created in your imagination. Use a separate sheet of paper to make notes about the event. You can use page 51 as a guide. Fill in the important information about this event below and on page 53. Using this information, write the news story in paragraph form.

Headline:_____

Main idea of story: _____

_____

_____

_____

_____

_____

Byline (name of reporter): _____

Dateline (date, city, state): _____

_____

Picture

Paragraph 1 (Lead paragraph)

The first sentence is dramatic. This paragraph provides a brief description that gives important information about *who, when, where,* and *what.* Then it explains *why* and *how.*

_____

_____

_____

_____

_____

_____

_____

_____

Lesson 1: The News Story

Activity 2—Writing a News Story *(cont.)*

Paragraph 2

This paragraph tells other important information.

_____

_____

_____

_____

_____

Paragraph 3

This paragraph provides additional details. Remember to begin a sentence with a quotation, a dramaic word picture, a summary stating the facts, or a question.

_____

_____

_____

_____

_____

Checklist for a Good News Story

Review the news story you have written, using the checklist shown below. Be sure that you can answer *yes* before you place a check (✓) next to each question.

○ Is my headline clear and interesting?   ○ Are my news sources cited?

○ Is my story organized correctly?   ○ Are direct quotations used?

○ Are my spelling and grammar correct?   ○ Is my story clear?

Lesson 2: Author/Poet Corner

Writing a Fantasy

What to Do:

❑ Complete the class pre-writing activities, as directed by the teacher.

❑ Review the basic structure of a fantasy, using the information shown below.

❑ Complete the outline and first draft of your fantasy (pages 57–59) on the basis of the pre-writing activities.

❑ Obtain constructive criticism by having a partner, group, or class respond to your writing.

❑ Revise, edit, and recopy your writing based on the responses.

❑ Save your fantasy for publication in the classroom newspaper.

Activity 1a—Basic Structure of a Fantasy

Carefully study the steps below before writing a fantasy.

---

1. Create an **opening** that . . .
   . . . captures the reader's attention.
   . . . introduces the main characters.
   . . . provides the setting (scene).
   . . . presents the problem.

2. Develops a **middle** that . . .
   . . . tells more about the main characters and the problem(s) they face.
   . . describes how the characters are trying to solve the problem(s).

3. Write a **climax** that . . .
   . . . demonstrates how the problem is solved.
   . . . shows how the main characters have learned from the experience.

4. Provide an **ending** that is brief and draws the story to close, with no "loose ends."

Use pages 55–56 to plan your fantasy before you write it. Think about the characters you want in your fantasy. If it is helpful, draw a sketch of the main characters. Use page 55 to record words and phrases that describe each character.

Lesson 2: Author/Poet Corner

Writing a Fantasy *(cont.)*

Activity 2a—Developing Characters

Main Character(s)

Name:	Name:
Physical Description:	Physical Description:
Personality:	Personality:
Strengths/Weaknesses:	Strengths/Weaknesses:
Likes/Dislikes:	Likes/Dislikes:
Magical Powers:	Magical Powers:
Motivation:	Motivation:

Supporting Character(s)

Name:	Name:
Physical Description:	Physical Description:
Personality:	Personality:
Strengths/Weaknesses:	Strengths/Weaknesses:
Likes/Dislikes:	Likes/Dislikes:
Magical Powers:	Magical Powers:
Motivation:	Motivation:

Lesson 2: Author/Poet Corner

Writing a Fantasy *(cont.)*

Activity 3a — Setting and Other Relevant Information

Think about the setting of your fantasy. If it is helpful, draw a sketch of the setting. Then use this worksheet to record words and phrases that describe the setting and other relevant information.

Setting
(Where and When Most Story Events Occur)

Description of the place:

Sights—

Sounds—

Smells—

Weather—

Time:

Other Relevant Information

Riddles—Potions—Chants—Other Types of Magic:

Special Vocabulary:

Other Important Information:

Writing a Fantasy *(cont.)*

Activity 4a—Outline

Think about the plot of your fantasy. Fill in important information for each paragraph of your fantasy as indicated on the outline shown on pages 57-59. (If you need to refresh your memory about your characters, setting, and other relevant information, refer to pages 55-56.) After you have completed the outline, use it to write the first draft of your fantasy.

I. Opening

> *Provide exciting opening sentence — could be a question, quotation, exclamation, or description.*
> *Introduce the main characters — brief description.*
> *Set the scene — where and when*
> *Present the problem(s).*

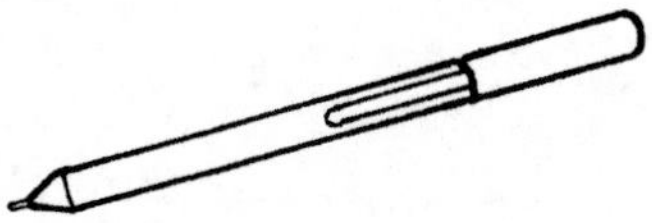

_____

_____

_____

_____

_____

_____

_____

_____

_____

_____

_____

_____

_____

_____

_____

_____

_____

Lesson 2: Author/Poet Corner

Writing a Fantasy *(cont.)*

Activity 4a *(cont.)* — Outline

II. Middle

Show interaction of the characters.
Explain the problem(s) in greater detail.
Describe how the characters are trying to solve the problem(s).
Build up to the climax.

_____

_____

_____

_____

_____

_____

_____

_____

_____

_____

_____

_____

_____

_____

_____

_____

_____

Lesson 2: Author/Poet Corner

Writing a Fantasy *(cont.)*

Activity 4a *(cont.)* — Outline

III. Climax

Show the characters solving the problem(s).
Explain what the characters have learned.

_____

_____

_____

_____

_____

_____

_____

IV. End

Be brief.
Tie up all loose ends.

_____

_____

_____

_____

_____

_____

_____

_____

Lesson 2: Author/Poet Corner

Writing Poetry

What to Do:

- ❑ Complete the class pre-writing activities, as directed by the teacher.

- ❑ Write the first draft of your poems (pages 61–63) on the basis of the pre-writing activities.

- ❑ Obtain constructive criticism by having a partner, group, or class respond to your poems.

- ❑ Revise, edit, and copy your poems based on the responses.

- ❑ Save your poems for publication in the classroom newspaper.

Activity 1b—"I Used to . . ." Poem

Not all poetry needs to rhyme. "I Used to . . ." is a non-rhyming poem. Think about things you did, thought, liked, or feared when you were young. Then think about how you act, think, what you like, or what you fear now. Complete the poem on this worksheet.

I USED TO . . .

I used to _____

But now I _____

I used to _____

But now I _____

I used to _____

But now I _____

I used to _____

But now I _____

I used to _____

But now I _____

I used to _____

But now I _____

Lesson 2: Author/Poet Corner

Writing Poetry *(cont.)*

Activity 2b — "I Dreamed"

Study the example of an "I Dreamed" poem in the box below. Notice the pattern used for this poem. Then use your imagination and the poem patterns below the example to write your own poem. You may wish to cut out the poem, mount it on construction paper, and add an illustration.

Example:

I Dreamed

I dreamed
I was a cat *(who or what — person or thing)*
Sitting under a shady tree *(where)*
Purring *(what is happening — action)*
Contentedly *(how the action happens — adverb or adverbial phrase)*

I Dreamed

I dreamed

_____ (who or what)

_____

_____ (where)

_____

_____ (action)

_____

_____ (how)

_____

Lesson 2: Author/Poet Corner

Writing Poetry *(cont.)*

Activity 3b — Rhyming Poetry

Brainstorm a list of some things or events that characterize each month of the year. Record your ideas on this page. Then use your list to write two rhyming lines about each month on page 63. An example is shown below.

> **Example:**
> In January there's lots of snow.
> With my sled, down hills I go.

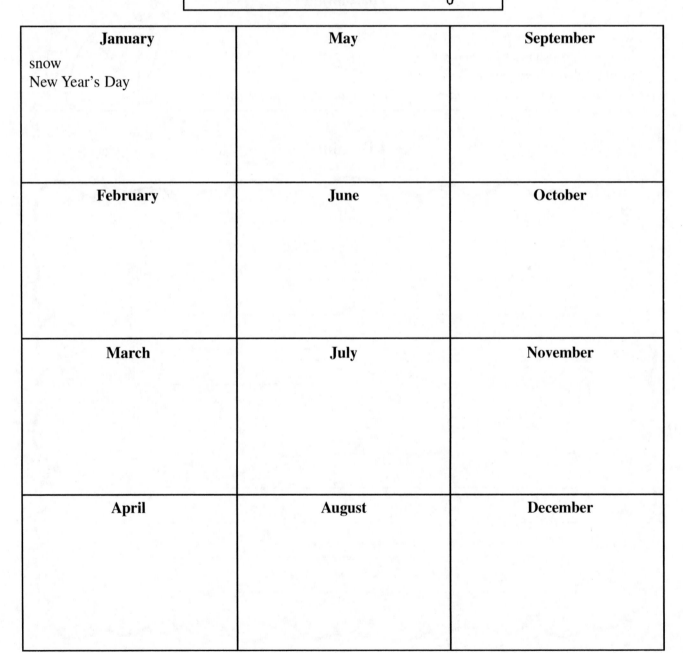

January	May	September
snow New Year's Day		
February	**June**	**October**
March	**July**	**November**
April	**August**	**December**

Lesson 2: Author/Poet Corner

Writing Poetry *(cont.)*

Activity 3b *(cont.)* — Rhyming Poetry

January

_____

_____

February

_____

_____

March

_____

_____

April

_____

_____

May

_____

_____

June

_____

_____

July

_____

_____

August

_____

_____

September

_____

_____

October

_____

_____

November

_____

_____

December

_____

_____

Lesson 3: Art Critic

What to Do:

❑ Complete the class pre-writing activities, as directed by the teacher.

❑ Write the first draft of your critique on the basis of the pre-writing activities.

❑ Obtain constructive criticism by having a partner, group, or class respond to your critique.

❑ Revise and edit your critique based on the responses.

❑ Recopy.

❑ Save your critique for publication in the classroom newspaper.

Activity 1 — Portrait Critique

Carefully examine the portrait you are going to describe. Use your observations and knowledge of the portrait to fill in the appropriate information in the paragraph frame (pages 64–65). Then write a first draft description about the portrait based on your completed paragraph frame.

Paragraph 1 — Physical Features

Sentence 1—Begin with two general descriptive adjectives followed by the name of the portrait, the artist's name, and the year or era in which the portrait was painted.

Example: _____ and _____ , the portrait of
_____(general adjective)_____ _____(general adjective)_____

_____ was painted by _____ in
_____(name of person in portrait)_____ _____(name of artist)_____

_____ .
_____(year/era painted)_____

Sentence 2—Describe the face and hair.

Example: His/her _____ , _____ ,
_____(texture)_____ _____(color)_____

_____ face is framed by _____ , _____ ,
_____(shape)_____ _____(length)_____ _____(style)_____

_____ , _____ hair.
_____(texture)_____ _____(color)_____

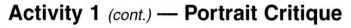

Lesson 3: Art Critic

Activity 1 *(cont.)* — Portrait Critique

Sentence 3—Describe the eyes.

Example: _____'s eyes are _____ ,
                  (name of person in portrait)   *(general adjective)*

_____ and _____ with a
            (size)   *(color)*

_____ expression.
      (general adjective)

Sentence 4—Describe the body.

Example: The subject's body is _____ and _____ with
                                  (height)   *(size)*

_____ arms and _____ legs.
          (adjective)   *(adjective)*

Sentence 5—Describe anything unusual.

Example: The unusual feature(s) of this _____is/are
                                        (man, woman, child)

_____ .

Paragraph 2—Clothing

Sentence 1—Describe the clothes.

Example: _____ is clothed in a_____ ,
            (name of person in portrait)   *(length)*

_____ dress/suit with _____ .
          (color)   *(trimming)*

Sentence 2—Describe the shoes if they are visible.
Sentence 3—Describe the headdress if there is one.

Paragraph 3—Opinions About the Portrait

Describe the emotional feeling the portrait gives you.
Tell how it ranks as a famous work of art and why.

Lesson 3: Art Critic

Activity 2 — Landscape Critique

Carefully study the landscape you are going to describe. Use your observations and knowledge of the landscape to fill in the appropriate information in the paragraph frame. Then write a first draft description about the landscape based on your completed paragraph frame.

Paragraph 1

Sentence 1—Begin with two general descriptive adjectives followed by the name of the painting, the artist's name, and the year or era in which the landscape was painted.

Example: _____ and _____ , the painting of
　　　　　　　(general adjective)　　　　　　　　*(general adjective)*

_____ was created by _____ in
　　　(name of person in painting)　　　　　　　　　*(name of artist)*

_____ .
　　　(year/era painted)

Sentence 2—Describe things that are notable about the landscape.

Example: In this work of art, one notices the _____

_____ .

Sentence 3—Describe any special features of the painting or unusual techniques used by the artist.

_____

_____

Paragraph 2

Describe what you find the most appealing about the landscape. _____

_____

_____

Tell how it ranks as a famous work of art and why. _____

_____

_____

Lesson 4: Interviews

What to Do:

❑ Complete the class pre-writing activities, as directed by the teacher.

❑ Write the first draft of your interview summary on the basis of the pre-writing activities.

❑ Obtain constructive criticism by having a partner, group, or class respond to your writing.

❑ Revise and edit your writing based on the responses.

❑ Recopy.

❑ Save your work as a reference for writing interview summaries for the classroom newspaper.

Activity—Taking Notes for an Interview

There are several things you can do to make an interview go smoothly. Review the following suggestions.

1. Be polite.

2. Stay calm even if the interview does not go exactly as you have planned.

3. Make an appointment in advance with the person you want to interview.

4. Be on time and prepared for the interview.

5. Practice asking for an appointment, as well as conducting the interview.

6. Take these things to the interview: worksheets (pages 67–68), sharpened pencil with an eraser, clipboard or book on which to write.

7. Avoid asking questions with "yes" or "no" answers. The best questions begin with *who, what, when, where, why,* and *how.*

Use the space on page 68 to take notes as you conduct the interview. After gathering all the information, use your notes to write a first draft summary of the interview in paragraph form.

Lesson 4: Interviews

Activity *(cont.)* — Taking Notes for an Interview

Person's Name: _____

Paragraph 1

Type of profession or job: _____

Length of time in this profession or job: _____

Responsibilities: _____

Skills required: _____

Paragraph 2

Positive points about job: _____

Negative points about job: _____

Would you recommend this job to others? _____

Why or why not? _____

Paragraph 3

Education: _____

Travel: _____

Interests: _____

Family: _____

Other interesting information: _____

_____

_____

_____

_____

Lesson 5: To the Editor

To the Teacher: Use this page as an introduction to editorials. See page 44 of the Teacher's Guide for information on this lesson.

The *editorial* is a special kind of newspaper article that includes both facts and opinions. It usually deals with a subject that causes strong feelings. The author of the editorial tries to persuade the reader to agree with her or him on the issue.

Sample Editorial Page

Page 2   Thursday, November 6, _____

GIVE STUDENTS A BREAK

Lunch recess may be a thing of the past for fifth and sixth graders if the Board of Education approves the proposed change at their meeting tonight. The change was proposed by Board Member Campbell who feels that in the United States students do not spend enough time in the classroom.

Students need a break! Recess helps them learn more! Research shows that vigorous activity and fresh air following a long period of indoor inactivity, sends a fresh supply of oxygen to the brain, relieving the sluggish feeling that often occurs.

The School Times urges the School Board not to eliminate recess for fifth and sixth graders. Students deserve a break and will return to the classroom refreshed and ready to get on with their learning.

> *THE SCHOOL TIMES*
> 122 S. Pernell Street
> Mooreside, IL 00000
> *Publisher:*
> E. Quentin Jones
> *Editor-in-Chief:*
> Theresa Smith

LETTERS TO THE EDITOR

Dear Editor:

I think our school should get a new mascot. The lion cub is too babyish. Maybe a grown-up lion would be better. What do other people think?

Sincerely,

Jay O'Connor

The editorial page should be in the same place in each issue of the newspaper, located on a special inside editorial page. A small masthead replica, which includes information about the publication and staff, is located on this page.

Find the following on the editorial page above. Mark and color code them as indicated below.

1. Name of newspaper (red)
2. Publisher (blue)
3. Editor-in-Chief (green)
4. Newspaper's address (yellow)
5. Three facts (orange)
6. Three opinions (purple)

Lesson 5: To the Editor

What to Do:

❑ Complete the class pre-writing activities as directed by the teacher.

❑ Write the first draft of your letter to the editor on the basis of the pre-writing activities.

❑ Obtain constructive criticism by having a partner, group, or class respond to your letter.

❑ Revise and edit your letter based on the responses.

❑ Recopy.

❑ Save your work as a reference for writing letters to the editor for the classroom newspaper.

Activity—Writing a Letter to the Editor

Choose a topic of concern to you. Fill out the important information concerning your topic on the worksheets (pages 70–71). From information on the worksheets, write the first draft of your three-paragraph letter to the editor.

Title

• Write a title that tells your topic of concern.

_____

Paragraph 1

• State the present problem/concern.

• List three or more facts concerning this problem/concern.

• Show how the facts support your opinion about the problem/concern.

_____

_____

_____

_____

_____

_____

_____

_____

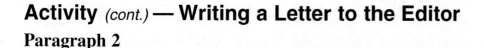

Lesson 5: To the Editor

Activity *(cont.)* — Writing a Letter to the Editor

Paragraph 2

- List at least two solutions to the problem/concern.

- Explain the possible consequences of using each of your solutions.

- You may wish to state what will happen if other solutions are used or if the problem/concern is ignored.

_____

_____

_____

_____

Paragraph 3

- Write a brief summary that restates the problem/concern and the changes that will result from using your solutions.

_____

_____

_____

_____

_____

Checklist for a Good Letter to the Editor

Review the letter to the editor you have written, using the checklist shown below. Be sure that you can answer *yes* before you place a check (✓) next to each question.

- ○ Does my title reflect my topic of concern?

- ○ Does my letter include at least three facts?

- ○ Is my opinion clearly stated?

- ○ Are my spelling and grammar correct?

- ○ Is my letter clear and concise?

Lesson 6: Writing Instructions

What to Do:

❑ Complete the class pre-writing activities, as directed by the teacher.

❑ Write the first draft of your instructions (page 73) on the basis of the pre-writing activities.

❑ Obtain constructive criticism by having a partner, group, or class respond to your writing.

❑ Revise and edit your writing based on the responses.

❑ Recopy.

❑ Save your work as a reference for writing instructions for the classroom newspaper.

Activity—Helpful Hints

Choose an activity for which you can write complete instructions. List the materials or ingredients that will be needed, write a list of steps for the directions, and then number the directions in the correct sequential order. (**Note:** if you need additional space, use the back of this page.) Use the information from this worksheet to write the first draft of your instructions on page 73.

Title: _____

Materials or Ingredients:
(List downward.)

_____   _____

_____   _____

_____   _____

_____   _____

Instructions:
(Write all the steps for the directions. Omit any unnecessary instructions. Add any omitted information. Then number the steps in the correct sequential order.)

_____

_____

_____

_____

Lesson 6: Writing Instructions

Activity *(cont.)* — Helpful Hints

Recopy the information from page 72. If you need more room, use the back of this page. Be sure to write the instructions in paragraph form, using the correct sequential order.

Title: _____

Materials or Ingredients:
(List downward.)

_____   _____

_____   _____

_____   _____

_____   _____

Instructions:
(Rewrite the instructions in paragraph form, using the correct sequential order. Time order words that may be used to begin sentences include the following: first, next, then, afterward, now, later, finally.)

_____

_____

_____

_____

_____

_____

_____

_____

_____

_____

_____

_____

_____

Lesson 7: Cure-Alls

What to Do:

❑ Complete the class pre-writing activities, as directed by the teacher.

❑ Write the first draft of your cure-all on the basis of the pre-writing activities.

❑ Obtain constructive criticism by having a partner, group, or class respond to your writing.

❑ Revise and edit your writing based on the responses.

❑ Recopy.

❑ Save your cure-all for publication in the classroom newspaper.

Activity—Writing a Cure-All

Choose something silly that you would like to cure. For example, if you have freckles you may wish to create a cure-all that eliminates freckles. Complete the information on this worksheet. Use information on this worksheet to write the first draft of one or more cure-alls.

Paragraph 1

Sentence 1 *(Tell what you want to cure.)*
Do you have _____ ?

Additional Sentences *(Describe the symptoms.)*
Do you feel _____
_____
_____
_____ ?

Paragraph 2

Beginning Sentences *(Write several sentences that describe the cure-all in detail.)*
_____
_____
_____
_____

Additional Sentences *(Describe the guarantee.)*
_____
_____
_____

Concluding Sentence *(Write an exciting/interesting concluding sentence.)*
_____

Lesson 8: Writing Reviews

What to Do:

- ❑ Complete the class pre-writing activities, as directed by the teacher.
- ❑ Write the first draft of your review on the basis of the pre-writing activities.
- ❑ Obtain constructive criticism by having a partner, group, or class respond to your writing.
- ❑ Revise and edit your writing based on the responses.
- ❑ Recopy.
- ❑ Save your review for publication in the classroom newspaper.

Activity—Reviewing Someone Else's Art

You can write a review about many things, including a performance or movie you have watched, an exhibit you have viewed, and a book you have read. Choose something you would like to review and that you think others will want to read about. Complete this worksheet to take notes for your review. Then use your notes to write the first draft of your review in paragraph form.

Paragraph 1

Title of what is being reviewed: _____

Author or producer: _____

Place to be attended, seen, or acquired: _____

Brief description of characters, performers, or type of artwork: _____

_____

_____

Paragraph 2

Brief description of the content: _____

_____

_____

Paragraph 3

Description of the best and worst parts: _____

_____

_____

Evaluation telling why you would or would not recommend it: _____

_____

Lesson 9: Travel Sections

What to Do:

❑ Complete the class pre-writing activities, as directed by the teacher.

❑ Write the first draft of your travel brochure on the basis of the pre-writing activities.

❑ Obtain constructive criticism by having a partner, group, or class respond to your travel brochure.

❑ Revise and edit your travel brochure based on the responses.

❑ Recopy.

❑ Save your travel brochure as a reference for writing travel sections for the classroom newspaper.

Activity—Writing a Travel Brochure

The purpose of a travel brochure is to tell people about a place in hopes that they will go there to visit. Think about a place that you like to go to and that you know well. Use your knowledge about that place to fill in the important information on this worksheet. Refer to the travel words provided by your teacher for ideas and correct spelling. When you complete the worksheet, write the first draft of your three-paragraph travel brochure, describing the place you have chosen.

Paragraph 1 *(Tell the name of the place. Describe the area. Describe how to get there.)*

_____

_____

_____

_____

Paragraph 2 *(Describe any or all of the following: places of interest, sports, entertainment, cultural attractions, the people. Tell about anything that will make people want to go there.)*

_____

_____

_____

_____

Paragraph 3 *(Describe the accommodations and prices.)*

_____

_____

_____

_____

Lesson 10: Survey Statistics

What to Do:

- ❑ Complete the class pre-writing activities, as directed by the teacher.

- ❑ Write the first draft of your survey report summary (page 78) on the basis of the pre-writing activities.

- ❑ Obtain constructive criticism by having a partner, group, or class respond to your writing.

- ❑ Revise and edit your writing based on the responses.

- ❑ Recopy.

Activity 1 — Sample Survey Report

Study the sample survey report below. Use the information to help you complete page 78.

Topic: Sports		
Question: Which is your favorite sport?		
Choices	Tally	Total
1. Baseball	~~THL~~ I	6
2. Swimming	I I	2
3. Football	~~THL~~ I I	7
4. Basketball	I I I I	4
	Grand Total	19

Summary: As a result of a survey concerning favorite sports of students attending Stanley Elementary School, it was found that football is the favorite sport, receiving 7 votes. The least popular sport is swimming, having received only 2 votes. A total of 19 students were surveyed, and each student appeared most certain of his/her opinion. It was not surprising that football was rated most popular since it is a well-publicized sport.

Lesson 10: Survey Statistics

Activity 2 — Survey Report Summary

Choose a topic you wish to survey. Write the topic in the top box of the survey form. Decide on the question you will ask and write it in the space labeled *Question*. List the four choices from which you want people to make their selection. Decide on the number of people you will survey. Conduct the survey and tally the results. Answer the questions at the bottom of the page based on the information from the survey. Then use the answers to the questions to write the first draft of your summary in paragraph form.

Topic:		
Question:		
Choices	**Tally**	**Total**
1.		
2.		
3.		
4.		
	Grand Total	

After completing the information in the survey, write the answers to the following questions.

1. How many people answered the survey?_____

2. Which choice received the most votes? _____ How many votes? _____

3. Which choice received the least votes? _____ How many votes? _____

Use the space below and the back of this paper to write the first draft of your survey report summary based on the answers to the questions.

_____

_____

Lesson 11: Advice Columns

What to Do:

❑ Complete the class pre-writing activities, as directed by the teacher.

❑ Write the first draft of your letter requesting advice and your reply letter on the basis of the pre-writing activities.

❑ Obtain constructive criticism by having a partner, group, or class respond to your writing.

❑ Revise and edit your writing based on the responses.

❑ Recopy.

❑ Save your work as a reference for writing advice columns for the classroom newspaper.

Activity 1—Writing to an Advice Columnist

Think of a personal problem you wish to have solved. Use this worksheet to plan a letter requesting help for your problem from an advice columnist. Write your plan on a separate sheet of paper. Then use the information from the plan to write the first draft of your letter requesting advice.

Street Number and Name

City, State, Zip

Date

Name of Recipient

Name of Newspaper

Address of Newspaper (City, State, Zip)

Dear Blabby,

Paragraph 1 (*State the problem in detail and tell exactly what has happened. Describe what you have tried to do about it.*)

Paragraph 2 (*Ask for advice on how to solve the problem. Be sure to thank the columnist in advance for his/her suggestions.*)

Closing,

Signature

(*You may use a word or phrase that describes you if you wish to remain anonymous.*)

Lesson 11: Advice Columns

Activity 2 — Writing a Reply

Pretend that you are Blabby, the advice columnist. Think of possible solutions to the problem you wrote about on page 79. Be sure your solutions show good judgment and are reasonable. Complete this worksheet to plan a reply letter that suggests one or more of these solutions. Then use the information to write the first draft of your reply letter.

_____ Name of Sender

_____ Street Number and Name

_____ City, State, Zip

_____ Date

_____ Name of Recipient

_____ Street Number and Name

_____ City, State, Zip

Dear _____ ,

Paragraph 1 *(Thank the person for writing you the letter. Restate the problem.)*

_____

_____

_____

_____

_____

Paragraph 2 *(Offer your advice.)*

_____

_____

_____

_____

_____

_____ , Closing

Lesson 12: TV Programs

What to Do:

❑ Complete the class pre-writing activities as directed by the teacher.

❑ Write the first draft of your TV program schedule on the basis of the pre-writing activities.

❑ Obtain constructive criticism by having a partner, group, or class respond to your schedule.

❑ Revise and edit your schedule based on the responses.

❑ Recopy.

❑ Save your work as a reference for writing TV program schedules for the classroom newspaper.

Activity — Writing a Schedule

Work with your class to complete the following information about a TV program.

Name of program: _____

Type of program (drama, comedy, sports, etc.): _____

Time of viewing (hour, day) _____ Channel: _____

Short summary of content: _____

_____

Recommendation (suitable age level, reasons for recommendation): _____

_____

Rating: Very Good   Good   Fair   Poor

Now think of a TV program that you enjoy and that you know well. Complete the information on this worksheet for that program. Then work with the class to create the first draft of a TV program schedule on the basis of the information that you and other students have written.

Name of program: _____

Type of program (drama, comedy, sports, etc.): _____

Time of viewing (hour, day) _____ Channel: _____

Short summary of content: _____

_____

_____

Recommendation (suitable age level, reasons for recommendation): _____

_____

Rating: Very Good   Good   Fair   Poor

Lesson 13: Classified Ads

What to Do:

❑ Complete the class pre-writing activities as directed by the teacher.

❑ Write the first draft of your "Job Wanted" classified ad on the basis of the pre-writing activities.

❑ Obtain constructive criticism by having a partner, group, or class respond to your classified ad.

❑ Revise and edit your classified ad based on the responses.

❑ Recopy.

❑ Save your work as a reference for writing classified ads for the classroom newspaper.

Activity—Writing a "Job Wanted" Ad

Think of a job that you could do well to earn some money. Complete the worksheets (pages 82-83), employing as many words as possible from the vocabulary list at the bottom of page 83.

Begin with a catchy headline phrase or question similar to the following examples. Then write the first draft of your classified ad requesting employment.

Example Headlines

Exceptional Employee	Do you need some time to yourself?
Self-Starter Looking for Work!	Are you too busy to do everyday chores?
Is your garden looking shabby?	Do you need a pet-sitter?

Headline

• Begin with a catchy headline phrase or question.

Paragraph 1

• State the services you will render. Be self-confident.

• State the reason why you should be hired and/or why you want the job.

• List your work experience and any additional skills that are important for this job.

_____

_____

_____

Lesson 13: Classified Ads

Activity—Writing a "Job Wanted" Ad *(cont.)*

Paragraph 2

- Give any necessary statistics.

  Name: _____

  Age: _____

  Phone number: _____

  Time available: _____

  Salary requirements: _____

Paragraph 3

- Provide two or three references.

Information	Reference 1	Reference 2	Reference 3
Name			
Position			
Address			
Phone Number			

- You may wish to request an interview.

Vocabulary for Writing "Job Wanted" Classified Ad

application	exceptional	organized	service
customer	experience	perfect	skills
dependable	guaranteed	positive	specialty
efficient	honest	punctual	successful
employee	interview	reliable	trustworthy
employer	motivated	satisfaction	unique

Lesson 14: Puzzles

What to Do:

❑ Complete the class pre-writing activities as directed by the teacher.

❑ Create the first draft of your word search puzzle on the basis of the pre-writing activities.

❑ Ask a partner, group, or class to solve your word search puzzle.

❑ Revise and edit your word search puzzle based on the responses.

❑ Recopy.

❑ Save your word search puzzle for publication in the classroom newspaper.

Activity — Making a Word Search Puzzle

Choose a topic — sports, food, pets, etc. Write your topic on the line provided below. Under *Word List,* write 12 words that are related to the topic you have chosen. Enter your 12 words on the *Word Search Puzzle* grid — one letter in each box. The words may be placed backward, forward, horizontally, vertically, or diagonally. Words with like letters may be overlapped. After you have written all 12 of your words in the grid, fill the empty boxes with letters selected at random.

Topic: _____

Word List   **Word Search Puzzle**

1. _____

2. _____

3. _____

4. _____

5. _____

6. _____

7. _____

8. _____

9. _____

10. _____

11. _____

12. _____

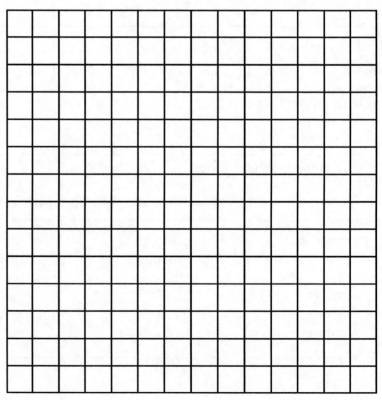

Lesson 15: Warnings

What to Do:

❑ Complete the class pre-writing activities as directed by the teacher.

❑ Write the first draft of your warnings on the basis of the pre-writing activities.

❑ Obtain constructive criticism by having a partner, group, or class respond to your warnings.

❑ Revise and edit your warnings based on the responses.

❑ Recopy.

❑ Save your warnings for publication in the classroom newspaper.

Activity — Writing Your Own Warnings

Think of a silly warning and write it in the space provided below. Give one or more reasons for your warning. Then write the first draft of your silly warning in paragraph form.

Silly Warning

_____

Reason(s) Why

_____

_____

Paragraph Form

_____

_____

_____

Now follow the same steps as described above to write a serious warning.

Serious Warning

_____

Reason(s) Why

_____

_____

Paragraph Form

_____

_____

_____

Lesson 16: Riddles

What to Do:

- ❑ Complete the class pre-writing activities, as directed by the teacher.

- ❑ Write the first draft of your riddles on the basis of the pre-writing activities.

- ❑ Obtain constructive criticism by having a partner, group, or class respond to your riddles.

- ❑ Revise and edit your riddles based on the responses.

- ❑ Recopy.

- ❑ Save your riddles for publication in the classroom newspaper.

Activity—Writing Riddles About People

Choose someone about whom you would like to write a riddle. The group of people you can select from include classmates; teachers; characters from movies, TV programs, or books; historical figures; and sports figures. Complete this worksheet to tell about the person you have chosen. Use similes to write more colorful descriptions. (Examples of similes: eyes as blue as the sea; skin as soft as silk; hair as golden as the sun.) The vocabulary list has suggestions that will help you choose a variety of words. Use your notes to write the first draft of your riddle in paragraph form.

Vocabulary for Describing People

agile	colorful	glamorous	lovely	shadowy
athletic	curly	gleaming	misty	shiny
black	dark	glowing	personable	shy
blonde	dazzling	golden	petite	starry
blushing	energetic	gorgeous	radiant	straight
bright	enormous	graceful	reddish	talkative
brunette	flaming	light	rosy	tall

Name of Person: _____

Description:

1. Describe his/her physical appearance (face, hair, eyes, body structure, etc.).

2. Tell something that this person is good at doing and/or for which he/she is famous.

3. Tell something that is special about this person.

4. Tell when and where this person lives or lived.

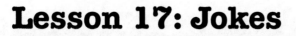

Lesson 17: Jokes

What to Do:

❑ Complete the class pre-writing activities as directed by the teacher.

❑ Write the first draft of your jokes on the basis of the pre-writing activities.

❑ Obtain constructive criticism by having a partner, group, or class respond to your jokes.

❑ Revise and edit your jokes based on the responses.

❑ Recopy.

❑ Save your jokes for publication in the classroom newspaper.

Activity — Writing Jokes for the Newspaper

Think about two of your favorite jokes. Use this worksheet to plan your jokes. Then write the first draft of your jokes in paragraph form.

JOKE 1

Topic Sentence: _____

Body of Paragraph:

Write several sentences that tell the sequence of events that build up to a climax or the punch line.

_____

_____

_____

Climax/Punch Line: _____

JOKE 2

Topic Sentence: _____

Body of Paragraph:

Write several sentences that tell the sequence of events that build up to a climax or the punch line.

_____

_____

_____

Climax/Punch Line: _____

Lesson 18: Comics

What to Do:

- ❑ Complete the class pre-writing activities as directed by the teacher.

- ❑ Compose the first draft of your comic strip (page 91) on the basis of the pre-writing activities.

- ❑ Obtain constructive criticism by having a partner, group, or class respond to your comic strip.

- ❑ Revise and edit your comic strip based on the responses. Be sure your comics appear in the format you have chosen.

- ❑ Recopy.

- ❑ Save your comic strip for publication in the classroom newspaper.

Activity 1 — Expressions

Look at these expressions. Read what each person said. Then draw a line connecting each person to the correct words.

"Look out below!"	"I stubbed my toe!"	"What a great new bike!"

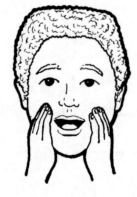

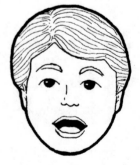

Lesson 18: Comics

Activity 2 — Making Your Own Cartoon

In each cartoon boxes below, write what you think the characters are saying. In the last box, draw your own character and add what the character is saying.

Lesson 18: Comics

Activity 3 — Comic Strip Situations

Think of a simple comic strip situation. Fill in the information below. Then complete Activity 4 (page 91) to create your comic strip.

- **List three or four characters. Give a brief description of each.**

  Character 1: _____

  _____

  Character 2: _____

  _____

  Character 3: _____

  _____

  Character 4: _____

  _____

- **Tell what the problem or conflict is.**

  _____

  _____

  _____

  _____

- **Write the sequence of events in a logical order for each frame.**

  1. _____

  _____

  2. _____

  _____

  3. _____

  _____

  4. _____

  _____

Lesson 18: Comics

Activity 4 — Designing Your Own Comic Strip

Use the information you wrote on page 90 to create the first draft of your comic strip in the boxes below.

Frame 1	Frame 2

Frame 3	Frame 4

Lesson 19: Advertisements

What to Do:

- ❑ Complete the class pre-writing activities as directed by the teacher.

- ❑ Review the information and samples from Activities 1–3 (pages 92–94)

- ❑ Write the first draft of your advertisement (page 95) on the basis of the pre-writing activities. Use the checklist (page 94) to evaluate your advertisement as you work on it.

- ❑ Obtain constructive criticism by having a partner, group, or class respond to your advertisement.

- ❑ Revise and edit your advertisement based on the responses. Then go over it with a dark pen.

- ❑ Save your advertisement for publication in the classroom newspaper.

Activity 1—Designing an Advertisement

Follow these basic principles for designing an advertisement.

1. Draw lines on which to write your information.
2. Make the layout simple.
3. Do not overcrowd the ad with too much text or illustration.
4. Use a dominant picture or headline which will attract attention.
5. Use a prominent headline stating the benefit of the product or service.
6. Make the ad complete by including these features:
    - description of article or service (size, color, prices, special features, etc.)
    - store/business name or logo that uses distinctive lettering or a design that identifies the advertiser
    - location
    - telephone number
    - hours
    - credit cards

Lesson 19: Advertisements

Activity 2—"Catching Your Eye"

A newspaper makes most of its money by selling advertising space. A full-page ad may cost thousands of dollars. An advertising manager is in charge of getting businesses to use the paper for advertisements. The sales staff must convince business people that the ad will increase their business since so many readers will see it. Once a company has decided to advertise in the paper, the advertising department's artists may help the business develop an ad that will catch people's attention and get them to buy their product.

1. Which ad "catches your eye"? _____

2. Which ad tells you where to buy the product? _____

3. Which ad tells you the store's hours? _____

4. Which ad gives you information that would help you if you wanted to ask some questions? _____

5. Which do you think is the best ad? _____

Lesson 19: Advertisements

Activity 3 — Checklists for a Good Ad

Planning Checklist: Before you begin to work on your advertisement (page 95), use the following checklist to help you plan it. Be sure that you can answer *yes* before you place a check (✓) next to each question.

○ Do I know what the topic of the ad will be?
Topic: _____

○ Do I know who I am trying to attract with this ad?
Audience: _____

○ Do I know what information is essential to the description of the article or service?
Description: _____

○ Do I know what my dominant element will be?
Dominant Element: _____

○ Do I know the store/business name or logo?
Name/Logo: _____

○ Do I know the location of the store/business?
Address: _____

○ Do I know the telephone number for the store/business?
Phone Number: _____

○ Do I know the hours of operation for the store/business?
Hours: _____

○ Do I know which credit cards, if any, the store/business accepts?
Credit Cards Accepted: _____

Working Checklist: As you work on your advertisement (page 95), use the checklist shown below to see if you have followed the basic principles for designing a good ad. Be sure that you can answer *yes* before you place a check (✓) next to each question.

○ Did I draw lines for all the written information?

○ Did I use a simple layout?

○ Did I leave an adequate amount of white space?

○ Do I have a dominant picture or headline?

○ Did I provide an adequate description of the article or service?

○ Did I name the store/business or show its logo?

○ Did I tell the location of the store/business?

○ Did I provide the telephone number?

○ Did I include the hours of operation?

○ If credit cards are accepted, did I show this?

Lesson 19: Advertisements

Activity 4 — Writing Your Ad

Use the checklists (page 94) to design your own advertisement in the space provided on this page. Begin by making a rough sketch, or first draft, in the *Practice Box*. Make changes according to the responses you get from those who look at it. Then use the other box to create the final draft of your advertisement. Trace over the lines of your advertisement with a dark marker.

Practice Box

Final Draft of Ad

Lesson 20: Sports

What to Do:

- ❑ Complete the class pre-writing activities, as directed by the teacher.
- ❑ Write the first draft of your sports article on the basis of the pre-writing activities.
- ❑ Obtain constructive criticism by having a partner, group, or class respond to your writing.
- ❑ Revise and edit your writing based on the responses.
- ❑ Recopy.
- ❑ Save your work as a reference for writing sports articles for the classroom newspaper.

Activity — Writing Your Own Sports Article

Recall a sporting event that you have recently viewed live or on TV. Record important information about that event on this worksheet. Then use your notes to write the first draft of your sports article. You may find the following vocabulary list helpful when writing your article.

Sports Vocabulary

athlete	commentator	finals	match	playoff	stadium
championship	competition	judge	official	referee	stands
coach	contestant	loser	opponent	spectator	winner

Paragraph 1

Name of the event: _____

Date of the event: _____

Name of the contestants/players: _____

Where played: _____

Final score: _____

Paragraph 2

Most exciting moments: _____

Paragraph 3

Star players: _____